0721

M000237452

LET THE FIRE BURN

Nurturing the Creative Spirit of Children

A Children's Book for Adults

LET THE FIRE BURN
Nurturing the Creative Spirit of Children

A Children's Book for Adults

Written by Vince Gowmon, CPCC, BBA
www.VinceGowmon.com

Illustrations by Anna Bradley
www.AnnaCartoons.com

© 2014 Vince Gowmon. All rights reserved.

Paperback ISBN: 978-0-9938595-0-2

No portion of this book may be duplicated or used in any form, by any electronic or mechanical means (including photocopying, recording, or information storage and retrieval), for any profit-driven or non-profit-driven enterprise, without prior permission in writing from Vince Gowmon. Brief excerpts may be shared subject to inclusion of this copyright notice, and with written permission from Vince Gowmon.

**Additional copies of this book may be ordered by visiting
www.VinceGowmon.com**

LET THE FIRE BURN
Nurturing the Creative Spirit of Children

A Children's Book for Adults

Written by Vince Gowmon
www.VinceGowmon.com

Illustrations by Anna Bradley
www.AnnaCartoons.com

*"The best way to preserve a child's vision
is to let them see things their way rather than yours."*

~ Dr. Jacob Liberman

To the fire that is in each one of us.
May it burn bright and light up the world.

Preface

Ever since I was a child, I have had a hard time fitting in with the norms of society. My parents would attest that I was not one who conformed easily. I always saw myself as different, but was never clear why I felt this way.

There was something burning inside of me that I could not put my finger on, and it would not leave me alone. It made it difficult to walk where others walked, believe what others believed, and act as others acted. It made me intolerant of social conventions and resistant of the status quo. It was a burning desire that made me feel there was more to life than what I was experiencing.

Simply put, I wanted more. And yet still, I continued to twist and turn, unable to find a place to stand. I was unhappy, confused and alone.

It was only after years of soul searching that I finally discovered that what I had been looking for was inside me all along. What I wanted was to feel and know the creative power and potential of my inner fire. I wanted its presence to flicker in my body and suffuse everything I said and did. And I wanted its joyful spark, and the gifts and talents it imbued me with, to light up my face, and the world.

Children want no different. They want to feel and express their creative fire as well. In fact, they do feel and express it, but sadly, they lose touch with it over time. They eventually succumb to social pressures, school expectations, sensory overload from the information age, and more. As a result, they become lost, angry and overwhelmed.

Children are hungering to have their creative spirit nurtured. They are hungering for it to be recognized and expressed. It is time we made tending their fire a priority. As we do, we will no longer have a society living in the shadows, desperately trying to fill a void that only the light of our fire can fill.

My intention in writing this book is for you to remember the joys and wonder of your fire, and for you to more easily recognize the fire in each child. I hope to reignite your creative power and potential, and to increase your faith in, and understanding of, how the fire speaks in each one of us. And I want the creative spirit of children to be nurtured more deeply in everything from parenting, to education and business. Children are our future, after all. They are the leaders of tomorrow. The health of humanity, and our planet, is dependent on their fires shining brighter than ever.

From my fire to yours,
Namaste.

Vince Gowmon ~ July 2014

LET THE FIRE BURN
Nurturing the Creative Spirit of Children

A Children's Book for Adults

Look at a child,
and you may see
a small,
dependent creation,
an innocent
without clarity
or direction.

But beyond our physical perception of the individual child living in our temporal existence, lies something *powerful* and *ineffable*, and more *magnificent* than the eyes can see.

Within each child
lies a *roaring fire*;
a fire built
from the
seat of the soul,
the
heart of the
universe.

This fire burns
with a *fierce desire*,
a *wildly joyous*
and *eager*
desire
to *create*,
to *play*,
to live to its
fullest *potential*,
and *carve* a path
across time
and space.

Its zest for life
must not be contained.
For this spark
is the lifeblood
of the child,
his very reason
for being here.

To douse the fire
is to empty the child
of his truthful content,
and to leave him
without a dream,
forgetful
of why he is here.

For within the fire
lies a *purpose*,
a calling
much bigger
than any
we could
prescribe.

It is a
creative potential,
a *creative force*,
borne from the
dawn of time,
from the depths
of all that has
ever been
imagined.

And it is ready
to be expressed,
ready to live,
and to shine
a new,
unique light
into the darkness
of our struggling
world.

It is why
the child is here:
to live
this inner truth,
to contribute
and serve,
and to feel
the *joy,*
passion,
and *love*
that comes with
having this fire.

And you have a role to play
in nurturing this fire.

Don't worry, though!
It's not about
figuring things out
for her.

Phew!

You don't have to
fill her mind,
lay out the map,
and plot the destinations.

At least
not as much
as we normally do.

She does not need
as much
structure,
direction,
and control.

At least,
not as much
as we have
traditionally given.

Because
it knows its Self!
The roaring fire
knows more
than you think.

Letting our
fire burn bright
is more of an
inside-out journey
that is meant to
be lived
by letting the fire
be the foremost
source of guidance.

Like all fires,
it needs space
to breathe.

For this fire blazes
with a tremendous
authority
that is decidedly
self-assured,
fierce in its
conviction,
clear in its direction,
and *understanding*
of its capacity.

It knows what it needs!
The roaring fire
knows more
than you think.

It is *whole*
and *complete*
in its essence.
It has
everything it needs
to fulfill
its purpose,
its reason
for being here.

It has a built-in
compass
that acts as the
ultimate guide,
the originating
source of truth.

It illuminates the
path in front,
and shines a light
on what it needs
and doesn't need.

It knows the way!
The roaring fire
knows more
than you think.

And please understand,
this is not an
intellectual journey.

The fire's path
is not rooted in
analytics,
plans,
systems
or forecasts.

It does not need
as much
intellectual stimulation
as you think.

Rather, it is a
journey of the
Heart.

A swirling,
colorful path
that moves
as a child moves –
in spirals,
twists,
and unpredictable
turns!

*Flames don't flicker
in a straight
line.*

While the intellect
can *serve* the
heart
with its maps
and analysis,
the heart -
the fire -
is ultimately the
master,
and the intellect,
the faithful
servant.

Less is therefore more
if you want to allow
the wild fire
in each child
to burn
to its fullest.

Less is more
if you want to
raise,
educate,
and generally support
the heart to
inhale and
exhale
to its
fullest capacity.

What the child
does need
is for you to
help him fulfill
his purpose
in a way that
nurtures the
heart,
and *respects* the
power and
inner guidance
of the fire.

It is one of the
sacred purposes
of being an adult -
to help a child
manifest his gifts and
unlimited potential.

To help him
live as an
authentic expression
of his fire
and be of service
to the world.

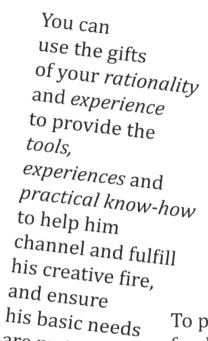

You can
use the gifts
of your *rationality*
and *experience*
to provide the
tools,
experiences and
practical know-how
to help him
channel and fulfill
his creative fire,
and ensure
his basic needs
are met.

This is one
important role -
the role of the
responsible adult.

To provide
food and shelter,
and point out possible
frameworks,
programs,
boundaries
and systems,
that can
support the
fire to breathe to its
fullest capacity.

But this role
has its limits -
especially if done
too much!

Because in being the
responsible adult,
we are more inclined
to just do
for the child -
to place a great deal
of our energy on
pointing and
providing.

It is not enough
to place so much
of our energy on
ensuring children
cross their t's,
clean their room,
and eat their meals.

Simply doing *for*
is not enough.
It is certainly
not enough
for the fire
to burn bright.

It is not enough
to just provide
intellectual capacity,
and ensure
they are safe
and secure.

This only provides
the *container*,
for the fire
to burn.

While important,
it is only the
fetching and laying
of rocks
for the fire pit.

It is not enough
because in only
doing *for*,
there is still
a separateness,
a disconnect,
an emptiness.

It is not enough
because *your* fire
has yet to be felt
by her.

You haven't
brought your fire
to the fire pit!

Only the spirit
of an adult
can nurture
the spirit
of a child.

Everything else
is just structure.

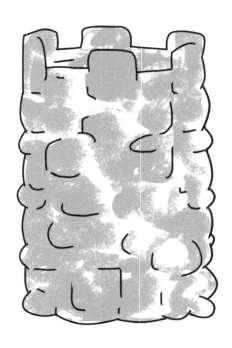

It is what we
imbue the
structure with
that touches the
human spirit.

Bringing your fire
to the fire pit
is, therefore, the other
sacred purpose
of an adult.

Letting it
be felt and expressed
in all you say and do,
in how you point,
and in what you provide,
is indeed your other
purpose!

*It begins with
awakening your
fire.*

Once you
awaken your fire,
you then find greater
balance between your
two purposes
as an adult.

Because now
you are not just
doing for,
but *being with*
as well.

You can be
with the
fire
of a child,
because you can
be with
your own
fire.

You can more
intuitively sense
how many rocks
to lay out,
and in what fashion,
without suffocating
the fire.

You know this
because you can
feel your own
fire.

*It
begins
with
you.*

It
begins with
awakening
your own
fire.

Once it is awakened,
you and the
child
are then
connected.

Your fires
meet,
perhaps for the
first time.

And
everything
starts
from
here.

Fire meets fire,
and you
fan the child's
flames
with your very
being -
your very
presence.

Fire meets fire,
and you
support the child to
open to her Self -
to her life -
and all the
possibilities
that lie within
and ahead.

Fire meets fire,
and you
travel with her
in her world,
in her own
unique reality.

You no longer
walk in front,
nor do you
walk behind.

You walk
beside the child.

You meet her
where she is
because you have
met your
Self.

From this place,
equality,
understanding and
trust are felt
more fully,
and a loving *dance*
of openness and
mutual exchange,
is created.

From this place of
togetherness,
the sacred purpose
of an adult
is more easily,
and enjoyably
fulfilled,
and
anything
is
possible!

Yes!

Now you can
play with children,
and *play along*
in their world!

One of the best ways
to support children
to burn their fire brightly,
is to gift them
with your
playfulness.

When you play
with children,
you share the
depth and brilliance
of your
inner child.

You find
simple ways
to be
silly
with them
and make them
smile!

You know that
it is the
simple moments of
delightful connection that
tickle their hearts
far more than
anything you could
plan for them.

When you play together,
you help children
cultivate their
imagination
by encouraging them
to see and consider things
from a variety of
perspectives.

You let them see
a tree as a spaceship,
a stick as a magic wand,
and a rock as a friend.

You cheer them on
to think
outside the box
and color outside
the lines.

You encourage them
to think and perceive
as a fire moves!

You inspire
them to be a
Creator -
to own their
inner artist,
and express it
magnificently
on the canvas
we call
eARTh!

You support them to
trust and
express their
spontaneous Self,
rather than relying
too much on their
analytical mind.

By playing
with children,
you help them
walk *lightly*
and have a
sense of *humor*.

It is then
easier for them to
laugh at themselves
and not take life
too seriously.

When we
hold ourselves lightly,
we stay
connected to our
inner Light!

When you meet the
fire of children
with your own fire,
you shine your
light on them
by showing greater
curiosity.

Curiosity is the
art of expressing
genuine interest.

You are interested
in their fire
because you have
become curious
about your own.

You show interest by
regularly asking them
questions,
perhaps as many
as they ask
in a day!

You *inquire* about their
inner landscape,
including their
feelings,
desires,
concerns and
needs.

In fact,
you may ask them,
"What do you need?"
more often,
and then
follow their lead,
and *play along*
in their world.

You invite them
to show you
what's important,
where to go and
what to consider.

You encourage
them to seek
their own answers,
and be *explorers*
of their world.

You know
that the more
curious you are,
the more you give
their fire a voice.

And the more it speaks,
the easier it is
for the child
to hear and follow
its intuitive nudges.

When you
connect with the
fire of children,
and ask
many questions,
you tend to *listen*
more deeply.

You not only hear
the words children
are saying,
but also the feelings
behind their words.

You hear what they are
not saying,
and what their
heart wants to
express.

You tune into their
inner struggles,
and support them
to share what
they may have a
hard time articulating.

And you tune into
the excitement of
their desires,
and help them
expand and act
upon them
even more.

When you meet children
with your own fire,
you are also more
willing to let
them make
mistakes,
many mistakes,
and get
messy in life.

You know that
like a fire,
life does not
unfold in a
linear way,
but rather through
unpredictability,
and even
chaos!

As such,
you believe that by
embracing messiness and
*learning to learn
through* it,
children are better
prepared for our
rapidly changing and
uncertain world.

They will be
better able to
translate challenges
into *opportunities*
for growth and
empowerment.

After all,
we learn most
about ourselves -
our fire -
and life
when things get
messy,
not when things
are going
according to our
plans!

It's from within the
spaciousness of uncertainty
that the fire's wisdom
arises most often.

When your fire
meets the fire
of children,
you also place greater
faith in the
urgency of their
dreams.

You encourage them to
daydream,
and you inquire about their
night dreams.

You help them
dream *Big* and
play *Big*!

You help them
because you know that
through dreaming
they connect to the
limitless imaginings
of their
fire.

One dream
can be the spark
that directs them on to
many wonderful adventures,
and the fulfillment of
why they are here.

When you
meet children
in their dreams,
you more fully
allow them to
live with
joy!

Joy is an indicator
that we are
living in
integrity
with our
fire,
that we are
on the
right track
with our dreams
and
creative spirit.

Joy is our
fire's way of
saying...

That is because
joy is our
true nature.
It is the
essence of
who we are.

The more joy
you bring
to the fire-pit,
the more joy
children will want
to bring as well.

Joy begets joy.
Joy is *fuel*
for the
fire.

Joy
lights the way
for our
creative spirit
to shine!

"*Yes*!"

By meeting
the fire of children
with your own,
you humbly recognize
that their fire is
different than
yours.

Their flames
do not flicker the
same way yours do,
nor do they have the
same temperature,
intensity
or color.

Children's feelings,
perceptions,
desires and
talents
are specific to their
unique fire
and purpose.

And they are all a
reflection of
what they are
meant to learn,
and how their fire
needs to grow
or evolve.

To expect children
to be the same as you,
to have the same
goals, beliefs and opinions,
and to problem-solve
as you would,
is both illogical
and insensitive.

This is especially true
given that the world
they are growing up in
is vastly different
from the one that
you and I experienced
at their age.

All you can do is
accept
that they are
built differently.

Accept
that in the deepest
recesses of their fire,
they know.

And accept
that asking them
"What does your heart say?"
may be the wisest choice
you can make.

So play and
connect with
children
in their reality.

Let them feed
their fire
in their own
unique way.

And of course,
remember the
power and
beauty of your
own fire,
and share it
in its fullness.

By doing so,
you support children
in their direction,
rather than
steering them
in your
own.

Ah,
but to do so,
you must
let go
to some degree.

You must
let go of
control
to play along
and let children
lead.

You must
let go of
control
to assume they
know best.

You must
let go of
control
to stand in the
place of curiosity
and trust
their creative
process.

To dance
with a child's fire
is therefore no
small feat!

It takes
courage,
patience and
humility
to follow their
unique process,
and dance in the
unknown.

And it takes
vulnerability
to show
your true Self
and dance in
your own
unique fire.

This does not mean
you never have an
agenda.
As a parent, teacher,
or caregiver,
you will need to
take charge.
You will need to
point the way.

Nor does it mean that
you don't say
"*No.*"
There will be a time
to set boundaries.

It just means that
you are willing to
explore children's agendas,
follow their lead,
and say "*Yes!*"
more often!

The good news is that
it easier to say
"*Yes!*" to them
if you make
saying "*Yes!*" to
your own fire
a priority.

If you practice
immense *self-care*
and commit to the
journey of
inner exploration;

If you are curious
about your fire,
listen to its
intuitive nudges,
and courageously
act on its desires;

If you express your
creative spirit
and choose things
that bring you joy;

If you regularly
spend time in
silence,
in the solitude of
nature,
self-reflecting and
connecting
within.

It is easier to say "*Yes*!"
if you spend time with
people who
feed your fire
with their own,
and release those things
and people that
dampen your flame.

If you are *willing* to
stand in the fullness
of your own fire,
even if those around you
question, doubt and challenge
your inner truth and
conviction;

If you are willing to
let the fire burn away
who you think you are
and "should" be,
and all
that is not true

in your self
and your life;

If you are willing to
stand naked
in the *emptiness*,
when all has
fallen away,
open,
receptive and
vulnerable.

Only then
can you be a
loving dance partner
in Life's grand
interplay!

Only then
can you dance
with the fire
of a child.

Only then
can you
welcome in
who you really
are.

And…
there is one more thing.

It is also easier to let go
if you remember...

We are not doing it alone.

There is something
grander, vaster,
more intelligent
at play here.

We are *co-creating*
with something greater
than our individual
self.

Our flame is connected
to a larger Flame
that is the
wholeness of Life,
the entirety of the cosmos,
the collective Dreamer
of all dreams.

It is the higher,
orchestrating Intelligence
that contains,
binds,
and imbues
all parts,
all systems,
all minds,
and all hearts.

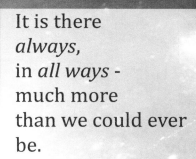

It is there
always,
in *all ways* -
much more
than we could ever
be.

It is the One
that is ultimately
in charge.

It is the One,
that holds
the container
for the fire
to burn.

It is the One
that is the
ultimate provider,
and originating Source
of the fire.

More and more,
the children
who are born
into the world today
know this.

They know this
Source,
this One,
intrinsically.
They feel it
deep inside.

Even if they
cannot quite name it,
they feel it
because they have
fires that burn
stronger than
ever.

Have you noticed that,
increasingly,
children are
restless;
that they are less
willing to accept
the status quo?

They want *more*!
They want things
that are different
from what you and I
wanted when we were
their age.

They sense
they are here
to do something
bigger
than what our world
currently offers
and encourages.

And they
won't
settle
for less.

Therefore,
it is our purpose,
our *sacred purpose*
as adults,
to release the child
to his fire,
release the child
to Life,
and know
he is taken care of.

He is loved,
more than we will
ever know.

It is our
sacred purpose
to have *patience*
with her timing,
and be *understanding*
of her unique
needs and choices.

Most children and youth
need time
to get clear
on how their fire
is meant to
manifest.

While they can
feel it within,
they may not
immediately or easily
recognize how it is
meant to look
without.

Their fire's presence
causes them
to travel along
unconventional *zigzag* paths
and experience
unconventional challenges,
guessing and testing,
searching for its
full expression.

So whether you are a
parent,
teacher
or caregiver,
they require
lots of support
from you.

Specifically,
they need you to
travel with them
in their
zigzag reality,
and
expose them to as many
diverse experiences as
possible.

From playing instruments,
to listening to music;

From climbing mountains,
to swimming in the ocean;

From painting and drawing,
to building sandcastles
and tree forts;

From creating mud pies,
to discovering sea shells;

From dancing and singing,
to playing board games;

From making up fairy tales,
to reading juicy novels...

children are *natural explorers.*

They need to
exercise this
innate impulse
so they can sense
what resonates
with their fire,
and makes them
come alive!

They are not meant
to be limited to the
3 R's
in the same way
they are not meant
to be bound to a
desk or technology
all day long.

The child's fire
is a wildly
creative,
adventurous and
expressive
spirit!

The more they
can explore,
the better the chance
sparks will fly,
and their fire
will scream
"Yes!"

And with you
by their side,
you can help
identify those
moments of aliveness,
and encourage
children to explore
them further -
if they choose.

Don't be attached, though,
to those moments.
Don't be attached to
how strong the
flames are,
or to how long
they last.

Sometimes a
spark is lit,
which is of course
wonderful!
But then it may
suddenly go out.

The fire is *dynamic*
after all,
not static!
It rises and falls as
feelings,
tastes and
appetites change.

So be patient.
Trust the
unfolding,
and let them
explore.

This will help you
release your need for
a particular spark
to point to
what they will do
when they grow up.

It will
allow you to be more
present to,
and appreciative of,
how the
fire is speaking
in the
everyday little
moments.

It will then be easier
to let the
little moments
lead to the
big moments
over time.

Bit by bit,
the fire will
reveal itself
on its own
terms.

In the meantime,
many children
may be confused
and frustrated
by trying to
align their fire
with their life.

They may struggle with
societal norms,
being different,
and not fitting in.

They may feel
tired of trying to
express their fire
in a world
that does not
recognize it.

It is not easy
to bring a
powerful, infinite fire
into a myopic, finite
world.

It is not easy
when humanity is
expected to
walk the
straight line.

It is not easy
when we are
taught to give
our power away,
and
listen more to others
than to ourselves.

It is not easy
when we feel safer
with our fires dimmed,
than when they are
fully expressed.

That is why
it is so important
that we
meet a child's fire
with our own.

Then we can
climb into his
experience,
and feel
what he is
feeling.

Then we can
meet him with
compassion and
understanding,
rather than our own
fears,
concerns,
and thoughts
on what we think
he "should" do.

Then we can
champion his spirit
on his terms,
rather than our
own.

From our fire to his,
we can then
love him more
unconditionally,
and relate with greater
humility.

This is not
easy to do, though,
if we are not
nurturing our fire
to the same extent
that children
want to nurture
their own.

And why should we?

We have not been
taught or encouraged to
any more than they have.
And few, if any, have
modeled this for us.

We left the dream
of our fire
many years ago.

Since time immemorial,
humanity has
forsaken its fire
and forgotten
why it is here.

Humanity has been
asleep,
separate from the
wakefulness of its
fire.

We therefore have
resistance to,
and judgment of,
a child's fire.

We cannot hold space
for its voice,
or be the
midwives
of its dreams.

That is why
it is paramount
that we begin
acknowledging
our fire
and letting it burn
today!

We can then
not only fulfill
our sacred purpose
for the
children in our life,
but also for
ourselves!

We can
nurture their
creative spirit,
and our own.

By following them,
they remind us of
who we are.

They become
the teachers,
and we
the humble
students.

Their fire
speaks to our own.
And the voices
of our fires
increasingly feed
one another,
and strengthen
together.

The voices of
our fires
are heard
and honored
within and
without.

And the
voice of the
greater whole,
the One Fire,
is thus
spoken for.

It is spoken
through you
and the child,
and out into the
world.

And the
tide of the
collective fire
rises.

From
light to light,
gifts of humanity
are then
illuminated,
and purposes
fulfilled.

From
love to love,
the planet's
sentient beings
are increasingly
nurtured.

And soon
a new world
is born.

It begins
with
you.

Only if we
let the fire burn
can we
remember
why we are
here.

Only if we
let the fire burn
can we
recognize and
nurture
the fire in
others.

Only if we
let the fire burn
can we
light the
shadows
of our
collective dream.

Only if we
let the fire burn
can we
be our
loving and
creative
Selves.

Only if we
let the fire burn
can we
be
set
free.

Only if we
let the fire burn.

Acknowledgements

This book has come about because of the love, generosity and expertise of many who allowed my fire to burn bright.

I start by thanking Dr. Jacob Liberman for kindly granting permission to include his quote from *Wisdom From An Empty Mind* (2001, Empty Mind Publications, www.jacobliberman.org), one of my favorite books of all time.

Thank you Susan Chambers for your proficient copyediting, and for your support in my decision to self-publish.

Judy Cashmore, Adam Cashmore Carr, Kate Toye, Griffin Toye-Oesch, Lynda Austin, and Judy Hillier, you have been so generous in giving me time out of your hectic lives. Thank you dearly for reviewing my book, and offering insightful and practical feedback.

Anna Bradley you have been such a gift. Your creativity is off the charts, and your passion for the arts is palpable. Thank you for bringing color, structure and feeling in the form of cover and interior illustrations, and the book layout. You are magical!!

I wouldn't be writing this book without all the people who have attended my playshops and keynotes. You have been such important teachers in my journey. This book has come about because of what I have learned from you. Thank you dearly for sharing your stories, challenges, joys and dreams.

Finally, I thank my family. From the moment I began the path as a Life Coach and Presenter, I felt your ceaseless love and support. You have fully championed my message, celebrated with me in my times of joy, and stood by me in my darkest hours. Thank you for walking beside me as my fire burned stronger.

With love and gratitude, thank you all!

About the Author

Vince Gowmon, CPCC, BBA, is the founder of Remembering to Play Events, and is a Certified Professional Life Coach. A popular speaker, he leads inspiring keynotes and playshops internationally for organizations and communities on topics such as Leadership, Intuition, Communication, and Play. People regularly comment on how uniquely fun and interactive his sessions are, and how applicable the skills are to work and life. Vince also provides individual and team phone/Skype coaching on all personal and professional matters.

Vince lives in beautiful Vancouver, Canada, where you will frequently find him on the mountains, in the ocean, or on a dance floor.

For more information on Vince, or to contact him, visit his website at **www.VinceGowmon.com.** You can also connect with him on Facebook at Remembering to Play Events, on Twitter at @VinceGowmon, and on LinkedIn and YouTube at Vince Gowmon.

About the Illustrator

Anna Bradley is a versatile Vancouver-based illustrator with a background in animation, cartoons and comics. Specializing in expressive character drawing, Anna lives for telling stories with heart about quirky individuals and exciting adventures. She specializes in creatively tailoring her works to the personalized vision of her clients, bringing playfulness, innovation, and insight. Her creativity results in the unique visual expression of both client and artist.

See examples of her fabulous creative works by visiting **www.AnnaCartoons.com.** If you have a collaborative project in mind, contact Anna directly at msannabradley@gmail.com.

CPSIA information can be obtained at www.ICGtesting.com
Printed in the USA
LVOW02s0905140115

422764LV00001B/1/P

9 780993 859502